Julius Caesar and the Roman Empire

How to Conquer the World: Book 1

By Peter Hollins

Table of Contents

Introduction: The Shadow of the Statues

To look upon the history of the late Roman Republic is to gaze into a mirror that has been shattered and reassembled a thousand times, each shard reflecting a different version of the truth. If you were to stand today amidst the sun-bleached skeletons of the Forum, you would find yourself surrounded by a silence that was once a roar. The air here carries a peculiar weight, a stillness that seems to press against the skin. You might watch the way the amber light of a fading Italian afternoon catches the jagged edges of the marble husks, or how the long, violet shadows of the Palatine Hill begin to stretch across the dust of the Via Sacra. These ruins are aesthetic to the modern eye—a collection of pleasing geometries against a brilliant Mediterranean sky—but they are also the graveyard of an idea.

The idea was that a city could be a world, and that a man could be a god. To the Romans of the first century BC, this landscape was not one of silent stone, but of terrifying, unstable vitality. It was a world where the old gods were fading into the background, and the law was becoming a fragile ghost. We often tell the story of Rome's fall as a series of cold dates and distant battles, a linear descent from republican virtue into imperial vice. But the truth is far more intimate, far more visceral, and far more haunting. The collapse of the Republic was not a sudden catastrophe that arrived like a summer storm; it was a slow, rhythmic unraveling of a shared reality.

It was the story of a civilization that had outgrown its own skin. Picture a city-state built for the management of small Italian valleys suddenly finding itself the master of the world, clutching the governing tools of a small town while presiding over a global superpower. In the friction between these two realities, a specific kind of atmospheric pressure began to build. You can almost feel it in the historical record—a heavy, thrumming tension, like the air before a lightning strike. It was a pressure that required a specific kind of man to vent it, a man who could navigate the narrow, filth-strewn alleys of the Subura as easily as the polished marble halls of the Senate.

This book is an attempt to walk the corridors of that collapsing world, to feel the grit of the Roman streets beneath our feet and the metallic tang of blood in the air. We are not here merely as observers, but as witnesses to a psychological synthesis that would fundamentally rewire the Western imagination. Before we reach the crossing of the Rubicon or the mud-soaked fortifications of Alesia, we must first understand the fundamental instability of the Roman soul. These were a people haunted by their own success, besieged by the very wealth and power they had fought for centuries to attain. They lived in a landscape of extreme contrasts, where the most refined Greek philosophy was discussed in rooms just feet away from places where desperate men sold their children into slavery to pay a debt.

In these pages, we will explore the three traits that allowed one man to navigate this storm: an audacity that saw social rules as mere suggestions, a mastery of narrative that turned the Latin language into a siege engine, and a tactical mind that viewed every aspect of human existence—from the bedchamber to the battlefield—as part of a single, unified strategy. We call this the "Caesarean Synthesis." It was a blueprint for power that did not just replace the Republic; it created a template for leadership that would be mimicked by every kaiser and tsar for the next two thousand years.

But before the synthesis, there was the man. And before the man, there was the city. As we move into Chapter 1, we must strip away the indifferent gaze of the museum busts and the sterile silence of the galleries. We must remember that these ruins were once vibrant, terrifying, and loud. We must see the black smoke rising from the wooden tenements and hear the desperate whispers in the shadows of the temples. We are entering a world where the old certainties are rotting from within, replaced by a hungry, restless energy. The journey begins in the long shadows of a city that had forgotten how to be free, and in the heart of a young man who was about to show them exactly what that loss would cost. It is a story of how a civilization ends—not with a whimper, but with the measured, rhythmic tread of a single man's boots.

Chapter 1: The Inheritor of Chaos (100 BC – 60 BC)

If you were to stand today in the center of Rome, amidst the sun-bleached skeletons of the Forum, you would find yourself surrounded by a silence that was once a roar. The marble husks of the Curia and the Rostra stand as monuments to a peculiar kind of ghost—a ghost of an idea. It is the idea that a city could be a world, and that a man could be a god. To the modern visitor, these ruins are aesthetic—a collection of pleasing geometries against a Mediterranean sky. But to the Romans of 100 BC, this landscape was one of terrifying, unstable vitality. To understand the rise of Gaius Julius Caesar, we must first look at the world into which he was born—a world where the old certainties were rotting from within, replaced by a desperate, hungry energy that would eventually consume the state itself.

Rome was no longer the small, stoic city-state of Cincinnatus, a place of farmer-soldiers and stern republican virtues. It had become a bloated, vibrant, and deeply traumatized superpower. It was a city of a million souls, a human anthill packed into high-rise wooden tenements—*insulae*—that frequently collapsed under their own weight or vanished in midnight conflagrations. In the narrow alleys, the stench of the Subura's open sewers and the metallic tang of blood from the nearby butcher shops mingled with the expensive, cloying incense drifting down from the Palatine Hill. It was a world of extreme contrasts, where the most refined Greek philosophy was discussed in rooms just feet away from places where desperate men sold their children into slavery to pay a debt.

The Education of a Fugitive

Caesar was born into the *Gens Julia*, a family of the ancient patrician aristocracy who claimed descent from the goddess Venus herself. Yet, by the time of his birth, the family's prestige was largely a matter of ink and parchment. Their wealth had evaporated, and their political influence had withered into a quiet, respectable obscurity. They lived not in a sprawling villa with marble peristyles, but in a modest house tucked away in the Subura. For Caesar, this proximity to the "common" Rome was not a burden, but a secret education. While his peers on the Palatine looked down at the Subura with a mixture of fear and disgust,

Caesar felt the thrum of its energy. He walked the same uneven cobblestones as the vegetable sellers, the weavers, and the veteran soldiers. He understood early that the heart of Rome didn't beat in the polished marble of the Senate house, but in the crowded alleys where the grain was sold and the rumors were traded.

His formal education was under Marcus Antonius Gnipho, a brilliant, freed slave from Gaul. In the quiet of his study, Gnipho would have drilled the boy in the art of the *controversia*—the ability to argue any side of a point with equal fervor. Gnipho taught him the power of the Latin language not just as a means of communication, but as a weapon of precision. But outside the schoolroom, the air was thick with a different kind of rhetoric. The Rome of Caesar's youth was a city defined by two men: Gaius Marius, the populist general who had saved Rome from the Germanic tribes, and Lucius Cornelius Sulla, the aristocratic traditionalist. They were the architects of a new kind of Roman politics—one where the legionary's loyalty was no longer to the abstract concept of the State, but to the General who promised them land and silver.

When Caesar was only thirteen, his aunt Julia married Marius. Suddenly, the faded Julii were at the center of a whirlwind. He watched as his uncle-in-law seized the city in a wave of populist fervor, and then watched as Sulla marched his army through the gates of Rome—the first time a Roman general had ever turned his blades upon the Mother City. The young Caesar walked streets where the severed heads of senators were displayed on the Rostra like grisly trophies. Internally, he felt a strange mixture of horror and realization. He saw that the "ancestral ways" he was taught to revere were merely veils over a darker truth: in Rome, the Law was a fragile thing, a mere suggestion that could be swept away by a man with enough steel at his back. He felt the weight of his patrician blood, but he also felt the pull of the masses. He realized that a man who could lead both could be unstoppable.

When Sulla returned from the East to claim the title of Dictator, he set about "purifying" the city through the proscriptions. These were not just killings; they were a bureaucratic liquidation of the opposition. Lists of names were posted in the Forum; anyone on them was a legal non-person, and their killers were rewarded from the state treasury. Caesar, now eighteen and married to Cornelia, the daughter of a high-ranking Marian, found himself in the crosshairs. Sulla ordered Caesar to divorce his wife as a sign of submission. It was a test of the soul. In a world where men were betraying their own fathers to escape the lists, Caesar looked the most powerful man in the world in the face and said no.

Behind that "no" was a cold, burgeoning pride. He felt that to submit to Sulla was to admit that he was a lesser man, a mere pawn in another's game. He was stripped of his inheritance and forced to flee into the Sabine mountains. Watching the distant glow of Rome from a damp mountain hideout, his resentment hardened into a singular, icy purpose. He was a man who had lost everything before he had truly begun, yet he refused to bend. He spent nights in the mountain rain, his skin hot with malarial fever, listening for the sound of Sulla's bounty hunters. Every snap of a twig was a potential death sentence, yet in this crucible, he found a terrifying clarity. He was not just a Julian; he was a Marius in the making. He learned that survival required a level of mental discipline that most men could not fathom, and he began to view the world as a series of obstacles to be circumvented rather than rules to be followed.

The Price of a Head

To escape the lingering, toxic shadow of Sulla's Rome, Caesar fled to the East, joining the staff of the governor of Asia. This was more than an escape; it was a period of observation. He saw how the provinces were bled dry by Roman tax farmers, and he saw the resentment building on the fringes of the Republic. It was during this period of self-imposed exile that he was captured by Cilician pirates—the undisputed masters of the Mediterranean trade routes. They demanded a ransom of twenty talents of silver, a sum they thought was kingly. According to the historian Plutarch, Caesar did not tremble. He laughed in their faces. He told them they clearly didn't know who they had captured, and insisted they demand fifty talents instead.

This wasn't just bravado; it was a psychological anchor. By demanding a higher price, Caesar was internally asserting his own value in a world that had tried to make him a fugitive. For thirty-eight days, he lived among the cutthroats as if he were their commander. He wrote poems and speeches and read them aloud to the pirates; if they failed to be impressed, he called them illiterate barbarians to their faces. He joined in their physical exercises, shared their rough meals, and slept soundly in their midst. Frequently, he told them, with a playful smile, that once he was free, he would return and crucify every one of them.

The pirates laughed, treating him as a charming, slightly mad mascot. But they did not understand the man. When the ransom arrived and he was released at Miletus, Caesar did not flee for the safety of Rome. He immediately used his influence to raise a small fleet, hunted the pirates back to their island stronghold, and captured them while they were still celebrating their haul. When the local governor, perhaps bribed or simply lazy, hesitated to punish them, Caesar took the law into his own hands. He ordered them all to be executed. However, as a final "mercy" to those he had shared meals with, he ordered their throats slit before they were nailed to the crosses. He felt no guilt, only the satisfaction of a balanced ledger. It was a lesson in the Caesarion method: a blend of high-wire charm and a total, unwavering ruthlessness that saw every promise—no matter how dark—carried through to the end. He stood on the shore, watching the silhouettes on the crosses against the setting sun, and felt the first true taste of absolute command. He realized then that power was not just given; it was taken, and then defended with a terrifying consistency.

The Ghost of the Temple

By 69 BC, Sulla was dead, and Caesar was beginning the slow, methodical climb up the *Cursus Honorum*. He was sent to Further Spain as a quaestor. This was a land of silver mines and rugged hill tribes, a place far from the sophisticated debates of the Forum. While visiting the city of Gades, Caesar came across a statue of Alexander the Great in the Temple of Hercules. He stood before it for a long time, the silence of the temple pressing in around him. Then, to the confusion and embarrassment of his staff, he began to weep. When asked what was wrong, he replied: *"Do you not think it is a matter for sorrow that while Alexander, at my age, was already king of so many peoples, I have as yet achieved nothing remarkable?"*

The tears were real, but they were fueled by a terrifying, internal clock. He felt the weight of his years like a physical burden. He wasn't just mourning his lack of achievement; he was terrified of being forgotten. This existential anxiety became his primary engine. He began to craft the myth of his own destiny, aligning himself not with the dusty traditions of the Senate, but with the world-conquering legends of the past. He was signaling to himself, as much as to the world, that his ambition was to change the map of history. He walked through the dusty Spanish provinces with a new intensity, seeing every bridge built and every tax collected as a step toward a much larger, bloodier stage. He began to study the mechanics of logistics and supply, the unglamorous underpinnings of Alexander's lightning-fast conquests.

Returning to Rome, Caesar realized that the old ways of gaining power—military glory alone—were being monopolized by men like Pompey the Great. To break through, he needed a different weapon. He chose the most modern of tools: debt. In 65 BC, Caesar was elected *Curule Aedile*. This office was usually a drain on a man's finances, but Caesar turned it into a massive investment in public opinion. He decorated the Forum with silver, and staged a gladiatorial show featuring 320 pairs of fighters in matching silver armor. The spectacle was meant to be overwhelming, a sensory assault that would leave the Roman people breathless. He was spending money he did not have, borrowing millions from Marcus Licinius Crassus.

Internally, this was a high-stakes gamble that likely kept him awake in the quiet hours of the night. He was walking a tightrope over an abyss of total ruin. But he found a strange thrill in the danger. By racking up such astronomical debts, he made himself "too big to fail." He felt a grim satisfaction in knowing that the wealthiest men in Rome were now his involuntary bodyguards. If he fell, their money vanished. He had turned his own vulnerability into a weapon of political invincibility. He had mortgaged his future to buy the present, and the Roman people loved him for it. They saw him as a champion who was willing to bankrupt himself to provide them with bread and circuses, not realizing that he was actually buying their loyalty with someone else's gold.

The Sacred Scandal

However, his rise was nearly derailed by a scandal in his own home. In 62 BC, Publius Clodius Pulcher was caught infiltrating the *Bona Dea* festival—a rite strictly for women—dressed in drag. His goal was allegedly to seduce Caesar's wife, Pompeia. The religious sacrilege was the talk of the wine shops and the baths. It was a disaster that could have destroyed a lesser man's dignity. Caesar felt the sting of the public mockery, the "cuckold" jokes whispered in the Forum. He could hear the muffled laughter when he entered a room, the pitying looks from his rivals.

But he refused to let emotion dictate his response. He did not accuse Clodius at the trial, not wanting to alienate a rising populist leader whose street gangs could be useful for the coming elections. But he divorced Pompeia anyway. When asked why he was discarding his wife if he refused to testify against her alleged lover, he gave his famous reply: *"Caesar's wife must be above suspicion."* Internally, it was a cold, surgical decision. He sacrificed his marriage to protect his image of untouchable rectitude. He had learned to view his private life as merely another theater of war, where sentiment was a liability and perception was everything. He had taken a personal humiliation and transformed it into a demonstration of his own untouchable standards, signaling to the Roman elite that even his family was secondary to the purity of his public image. He stood alone in his house after the divorce, the silence a testament to his commitment to the Great Game. He would be the hero of the story, even if it meant being a hero without a home. He realized that to reach the heights he sought, he had to become something more than a person; he had to become a symbol of Roman virtue, even as he worked to dismantle the Republic's foundations.

The Silent Conspiracy

By 60 BC, the pieces of the Great Game were moving toward a stalemate. Pompey the Great had returned from the East as a conqueror, but the Senate refused to ratify his settlements. Crassus, the richest man in Rome, was being blocked in his business interests by the conservative faction. And Caesar, returning from a successful governorship in Spain, wanted the Consulship—the highest office in the land. The Senate, led by the obstinate Cato, believed they could hold these men at bay by playing them against one another. They thought they could maintain the status quo by frustrating the giants, keeping the machinery of the Republic running through a series of petty vetos and procedural delays.

But Caesar saw the math of the moment. He felt a quiet contempt for the senators who thought they could manage him. He went to Pompey and Crassus and proposed the impossible: a private agreement to pool their resources and dominate the state. It was called the First Triumvirate. It was not a legal body; it was a conspiracy. Pompey provided the military prestige, Crassus provided the wealth, and Caesar provided the political brains. They met in secret, away from the prying eyes of the Forum, and partitioned the world between them. They realized that together, they were the state.

As the year 60 BC drew to a close, the Republic was still standing in name. Its temples were intact, its laws were on the books, and its senators still debated in the Forum. But the heartbeat of the state had changed. The center of gravity had shifted from the public assembly to the private dinner tables of three men. Three men now held the strings of the world, and they were pulling them in unison.

Caesar, the man who had started in the slums of the Subura, who had laughed at pirates and wept before Alexander, was now poised to take the Consulship. He had inherited a world of chaos, and he had learned to love the storm. He looked out over the city at night, the thousands of cooking fires of the Subura twinkling like a mirror of the stars. He felt a sense of arrival, but also a profound, restless anticipation. The speeches and the debts were merely the foundation. To maintain this position, he would need more than political maneuvering. He needed a war. He looked north toward the dark, unconquered forests of Gaul, a land that the Romans viewed as a wilderness of monsters and barbarians. To Caesar, it was a reservoir of potential glory, a place where he could forge an army that would be loyal to him and him alone. The inheritor of chaos was ready to become its master, and the first step of his march was about to begin.

Chapter 2: The Forge of Gaul (58 BC – 51 BC)

If you were to travel north from the sun-drenched marble of the Roman Forum in the year 58 BC, crossing the jagged, snow-dusted spine of the Alps, you would find yourself entering a world that existed in the Roman imagination as a realm of nightmares. To the Romans, Gaul was a vast, dark mirror of their own civilization—a place of endless forests, impenetrable swamps, and a people who seemed to possess a terrifying, primeval vitality. They called it *Gallia Comata*, or "Long-Haired Gaul," a land divided into three parts, inhabited by tribes whose names—the Belgae, the Aquitani, the Celts—carried the weight of ancient fears. This was the land that had once sent a war band to sack Rome itself centuries earlier, leaving a trauma in the Roman psyche that had never truly healed.

For Gaius Julius Caesar, now forty-two years old and finishing a controversial term as Consul, this northern wilderness was not just a threat; it was a necessity. He left Rome as a man with a fragile grip on power. Behind him lay a city of creditors and political enemies waiting for him to stumble. He needed more than just a victory; he needed a transformation. He needed the kind of wealth that could buy a city and the kind of military glory that could silence a Senate. He needed a forge, and in the sprawling, untamed landscape of Gaul, he found it.

The Migration of the Helvetii

The spark that ignited the Gallic Wars was not a grand invasion or a calculated act of aggression by a foreign king, but a migration. In the spring of 58 BC, the Helvetii, a Celtic people living in the high valleys of what is now Switzerland, made a desperate decision. Under pressure from Germanic tribes to the east and suffering from a lack of arable land, they burned their twelve towns and four hundred villages. They destroyed everything they could not carry, ensuring there would be no home to return to. A quarter of a million people—men, women, children, and elderly—set off in a massive, slow-moving column of wagons, seeking a new life in the fertile plains of the west.

To the modern eye, this was a humanitarian crisis of immense proportions. To Caesar, it was a *casus belli*. He was the governor of

Transalpine Gaul, and the Helvetii intended to march through his province. Caesar rushed from Rome to Geneva, reaching the frontier with the kind of speed that would soon become his trademark—*celeritas*. He arrived to find the Helvetii requesting peaceful passage. Caesar, playing for time while he gathered his legions, told them to return in two weeks for his answer.

During those fourteen days, he didn't wait; he worked. He supervised the construction of a nineteen-mile-long earthen wall, ten feet high, stretching from Lake Geneva to the Jura Mountains. This was Roman engineering as an act of diplomatic refusal. When the Helvetii returned, he informed them that "according to the custom and precedent of the Roman People," he could not grant them passage. When they tried to force their way across the Rhone, they were met with a wall of Roman shields and a rain of heavy javelins.

The Helvetii turned away, seeking an alternative route through the rugged territory of the Sequani. But Caesar followed them. He was no longer just defending a border; he was hunting a people. He chased the massive column across the landscape, a pursuit that lasted for weeks, the Roman legions marching through dust and rain, their pace dictated by the slow, creaking wagons of the migrants. Finally, near the town of Bibracte, the Helvetii turned to fight.

The battle was a horrific introduction to the reality of Roman warfare. The Roman legionary was not a soldier in the modern sense; he was a heavy infantryman designed for a specific kind of industrial-scale slaughter. Armed with the *pilum*—a heavy javelin with a soft iron neck designed to bend upon impact, making it impossible to pull out of a shield—the Romans shattered the Gallic charge before it even reached their lines. Caesar himself dismounted and sent his horse away, signaling to his men that there would be no retreat. He stood in the front ranks, the smell of sweat and iron thick in the air, watching as the Helvetian line broke under the weight of the Roman *gladius*.

The slaughter lasted until late into the night. The Roman accounts speak of a "mountain of wagons" where the Helvetian women and children made a final, desperate stand, hurling stones and spears at the advancing legionaries. When the sun rose, the Helvetii were no longer a nation; they were a broken remnant. Caesar ordered the survivors—barely a third of those who had set out—to return to their ruined homes in the Alps. He did this not out of mercy, but for a cold, geopolitical reason: he did not want the vacant lands to be occupied by the Germanic tribes from across the Rhine. He had won his first victory, but in doing so, he had signaled to the rest of Gaul that a new power had arrived—one that did not recognize the right of a people to move across the earth without Rome's permission.

The Enigma of the Third Person

One of the great frustrations for the historian is the wall Caesar built around his own mind. In his writings, he never uses the word "I." He is always "Caesar." This wasn't merely a stylistic choice; it was a psychological shield. By writing about himself in the third person, he was attempting to project an image of a man who was entirely in control of his emotions—a figure of pure, cold reason who existed above the fray of human fear. Yet, if we look closely at the letters he sent to his friends in Rome, such as the orator Cicero, we begin to see the cracks in this marble facade.

Behind the third-person mask was a man possessed by a restless, almost pathological anxiety. He was haunted by the memory of Alexander the Great, reportedly weeping at the age of thirty-three because he had achieved so little compared to the Macedonian king. In Gaul, this manifested as a frenetic need for activity. He was a man who could not be still. He dictated letters to multiple secretaries simultaneously while riding on horseback through the Gallic forests. He slept in a simple soldier's tent, not because he was humble, but because he was unwilling to lose a single hour to the comforts of a commander's villa.

His internal state was characterized by what the Romans called *dignitas*—a concept of personal honor and status that was more important to him than life itself. In his mind, every Gallic tribe he subdued and every bridge he built was a brick in the monument of his own reputation. When he felt his *dignitas* threatened by the Senate, his reaction was visceral. There are accounts of his temper flashing like lightning, his eyes— which contemporaries described as dark, piercing, and restless—burning with a terrifying intensity. He was a man who felt the weight of his debts and the shadows of his rivals every waking moment. This pressure did not break him; it refined him. He transformed his internal chaos into the external order of his legions. He was a man who had decided that the only way to escape the judgment of his peers was to become their master.

The Cult of the Tenth

It was during these early, brutal campaigns that Caesar began to forge a unique relationship with his soldiers, most notably the *Legio X Equestris*—the Tenth Legion. In the Roman military tradition, the commander was often a distant, aristocratic figure, a man of the Senate who viewed his troops as mere tools of statecraft. Caesar changed the script entirely. He called his soldiers "comrades" (*commilitones*) rather than "men." He knew their names, the names of their centurions, and the details of their families. He was creating a private society within the army, one whose primary loyalty was to him alone.

He practiced a form of "tactical praise" that was deeply psychological. He would single out individual soldiers for their bravery in front of the entire army, presenting them with gold torques and decorated shields. But he also demanded an unprecedented level of physical endurance. He marched on foot alongside them, often baring his head in the rain or the blistering sun. He ate the same hard tack and drank the same sour wine as the lowest recruit. Internally, he felt a deep, resonant connection to these men. He saw in them the same hunger for status and survival that had driven him from the Subura.

This relationship was tested to its breaking point during the campaign against the Nervii in 57 BC. The Nervii were a tribe of the Belgae, widely considered the most ferocious warriors in Gaul. They had no use for Roman luxury, forbade the import of wine, and lived in the dense, marshy forests of the north. They ambushed Caesar's army while they were in the middle of fortifying a camp on the banks of the river Sabis.

The chaos was total. The Roman lines were not even formed; many soldiers didn't have time to put on their helmets or uncover their shields. The Nervii burst from the woods like a tidal wave. In the center, Caesar saw his Fourth Legion wavering, their centurions killed, the standard-bearers falling. He didn't issue an order from the rear. He snatched a shield from a soldier in the back ranks, ran to the front line, and called out to the centurions by name, urging them to open up their ranks so they could swing their swords more effectively.

His presence changed the chemistry of the moment. The soldiers, seeing their commander standing in the thick of the blood and the mud, found a second wind. The Tenth Legion, which had been on the opposite flank, saw the danger their general was in. They charged back across the river, hitting the Nervii in the rear. The battle turned from an ambush into a massacre. The Nervii refused to flee; they fought from atop the mounds of their own dead until their nation was virtually extinguished. When the smoke cleared, Caesar had not just won a battle; he had created a cult. To the men of the Tenth, Caesar was no longer just a general; he was the man who had stood with them in the mouth of hell. They would follow him anywhere—even, eventually, across the Rubicon.

The Rhine and the Engineering of Fear

By 55 BC, Caesar's ambitions had expanded beyond the borders of Gaul. He looked toward the Rhine, the great water barrier that separated the Celtic world from the Germanic wilderness. To the Romans, the Rhine was more than a river; it was a boundary of the civilized world. Beyond it lay the Suebi and other Germanic tribes, peoples whom the Romans feared as giants of the forest. Two Germanic tribes, the Usipetes and the Tencteri, had crossed into Gaul, fleeing the pressure of the Suebi. Caesar met them with characteristic ruthlessness, slaughtering hundreds of thousands of them—including women and children—after a parley had already begun. It was an act of such blatant cruelty that back in Rome, his enemy Cato the Younger moved that Caesar be handed over to the Germans to atone for his "violation of the gods."

But Caesar was not interested in the Senate's morality. He wanted to project Roman power where no Roman had ever dared to go. He decided to cross the Rhine. But he would not cross it by boat. To do so would be to admit that the river was a barrier he could only traverse by the river's leave. He would build a bridge. He wanted the Germans to see that even the most formidable natural barriers were mere playthings for Roman engineering.

The Rhine was wide, deep, and fast-flowing, particularly in the early summer. Roman engineers had never attempted anything on this scale. Yet, in just ten days, Caesar's men constructed a timber trestle bridge nearly 400 meters long. They drove massive wooden piles into the riverbed at an angle, using a system of pulleys and pile-drivers mounted on barges. They built "upstream fenders" to catch the heavy trunks and debris that the Germans floated down the river in an attempt to break the structure. The sound of the pile-drivers echoed through the Germanic forests, a rhythmic, industrial heartbeat that signaled the end of their isolation.

When the bridge was finished, Caesar marched his legions across. He spent eighteen days in Germanic territory, burning villages and destroying crops. He didn't engage in a major battle; he didn't need to. The bridge was the message. It was a ten-day engineering miracle designed purely to intimidate. He had demonstrated that the Rhine was not a border, but a road for Roman feet. Once the point was made, he marched back across and dismantled the bridge behind him. He had conquered a river without losing a single man in combat. It was a masterclass in psychological warfare—a demonstration that Roman *technitas* was as lethal as Roman steel. Internally, Caesar felt a grim satisfaction. He had redefined the boundaries of the world, and he had done it through the sheer force of Roman labor.

The War of the Dispatches

While Caesar was campaigning in the mud of Gaul and the mists of the Rhine, he was fighting another war in the minds of the Roman people. Every winter, as the legions went into their camps, Caesar sat in his tent and wrote. These writings became the *Commentarii de Bello Gallico*—the Gallic War Commentaries.

To the Roman citizen in the Forum, these were not dense historical texts; they were dispatches from the edge of the world. They were written in a style that was deceptively simple—unadorned, direct, and written in the third person. By referring to himself as "Caesar" rather than "I," he created an air of objective authority. He wasn't just telling a story; he was reporting on the inevitable expansion of Roman civilization. He was the observer and the actor at once, a man who spoke with the clarity of a historian even as he carved out a new world.

The *Commentaries* served a dual purpose. First, they justified his wars. Under Roman law, a governor was not supposed to start new wars without Senate approval. Caesar framed every campaign as a defensive necessity—a response to a threat to Rome's allies or a pre-emptive strike against a rising barbarian tide. He was careful to mention the "barbaric" customs of the Gauls, the human sacrifices and the strange religious rites of the Druids, to ensure the Roman people felt their general was a civilizing force.

Second, they maintained his popularity. He described the exotic landscapes of Britain—the "tin islands" where the inhabitants dyed themselves blue with woad and drove chariots in a way that seemed to belong to the time of Homer. He described the strange animals of the Hercynian Forest—the elks that supposedly had no joints in their legs and had to sleep leaning against trees. In these dispatches, Caesar was the calm, rational center of a chaotic world. He was the commander who cared for his men, the engineer who mastered nature, and the protector of the Republic. By the time he returned to Rome, the people felt as if they had been on the campaign with him. He had turned the Gallic Wars into a national epic, with himself as the protagonist. The *Commentaries* were perhaps his most effective weapon; they ensured that while he was out of sight, he was never out of mind.

The Island Beyond the World

In late summer of 55 BC, and again in 54 BC, Caesar turned his eyes toward Britain. To the Romans, Britain was more than just a foreign land; it was a semi-mythical place beyond the Great Ocean that encircled the world. To cross the Channel was to cross the boundary of the known universe. It was a place of mist and shadow, where the sun supposedly set differently than in the rest of the world.

The first expedition was almost a disaster. Caesar took only two legions and had little knowledge of the tides. When the Roman ships reached the cliffs of Dover, they found the heights lined with British warriors, their bodies painted blue, their war-cries carrying over the sound of the surf. Caesar was forced to seek a landing further down the coast. As the heavy Roman transports ran aground in the shallows, the soldiers hesitated. The water was deep, the currents were strong, and the British charioteers were charging into the surf.

Then, the standard-bearer of the Tenth Legion stepped forward. He shouted to his comrades: *"Jump down, soldiers, unless you wish to betray the eagle to the enemy; I, at any rate, shall have performed my duty to the Republic and my general."* He leaped into the water, clutching the silver eagle. The soldiers, terrified of the disgrace of losing their standard, followed him. The landing was a chaotic, bloody struggle in the waves, but the Roman discipline eventually prevailed.

The war in Britain was a grinding, frustrating affair. The Britons practiced a scorched-earth policy and used their chariots to harass the Roman columns. Caesar marched as far as the Thames, even forcing a crossing, but he realized that Britain was not Gaul. There were no grand cities to capture, no centralized government to co-opt. The weather was atrocious, and a storm destroyed a large portion of his fleet at anchor. He eventually withdrew, taking hostages and extracting promises of tribute that would rarely be paid. Militarily, the British expeditions achieved little of lasting value. But politically, they were a triumph. The Senate was stunned. They decreed twenty days of public thanksgiving—the longest in Roman history. Caesar had done what even Alexander had not; he had crossed the Ocean. He had expanded the Roman horizon into the realm of legend, and in the eyes of the Roman mob, he was now a figure of mythic proportions.

The Scorched Earth

By 52 BC, Caesar believed Gaul was pacified. He was wrong. The various tribes of Gaul, after years of being played against each other, had finally found a leader who could unite them: a young nobleman of the Arverni named Vercingetorix. He was a man who had studied the Romans, perhaps even served alongside them. He understood that he could not beat Caesar in a pitched battle. Instead, he launched a total war of attrition. He ordered the "scorched earth" of Gaul.

"It is better," Vercingetorix told his people, "to burn our own homes than to allow the Romans to live off them." Twenty towns of the Bituriges were burned in a single day. The sky over central Gaul was black with the smoke of destroyed villages. The Gauls destroyed their own granaries and hayricks, intending to starve the Roman monster that had entered their house. For the Roman legionaries, the war turned into a nightmare of hunger and exhaustion. They were marching through a wasteland, their bellies empty, their boots worn thin.

Caesar found himself in a desperate position. His supply lines were stretched to the snapping point, and his allies were deserting him. He was no longer the hunter; he was the prey. The Roman army was forced to retreat, harassed at every turn by Gallic cavalry. Caesar's internal state during this period was one of immense pressure. He was watching his decade of work evaporate in a matter of months. But he did not panic. He remained the "master tactician," looking for the single mistake that Vercingetorix might make. That mistake came when Vercingetorix, perhaps under pressure from his own subordinates, decided to retreat into the hill fort of Alesia. He hoped to hold out until a massive relief army could arrive and trap the Romans from the outside. He had invited the Romans to a siege, not realizing that he had just stepped into a cage.

The Siege of the Two Walls

The response Caesar launched at Alesia was one of the most audacious feats of military engineering in history. He did not just besiege the fortress; he redefined the landscape around it. He built two lines of fortifications. The first, the *circumvallation*, was an eleven-mile ring of walls, ditches, and traps facing inward to keep the 80,000 Gauls in. The second, the *contravallation*, was a fourteen-mile ring facing outward to protect his army from the expected relief force of a quarter of a million Gauls.

Between these two walls, the Roman army lived and fought. They were the besiegers and the besieged at the same time. Caesar created a "death zone" of sophisticated traps: *cippi* (sharpened branches hidden in trenches), *lilies* (pits with sharpened stakes at the bottom), and *stimuli* (iron hooks buried in the ground). The Roman legionaries worked like demons, moving millions of tons of earth, their hands calloused, their faces caked with the red clay of Gaul. They were building a machine of war that covered miles of territory.

When the Gallic relief army arrived, the battle for Alesia became a struggle for the soul of the West. The Gauls attacked from both sides simultaneously. The Roman lines were stretched to the breaking point. The sound of 300,000 men screaming in the dark was a sound few Romans would ever forget. Caesar, wearing his signature scarlet cloak so his men could easily see him, rode from sector to sector. He was a blur of motion, his horse lathered in sweat, his voice hoarse from shouting encouragement. He knew that if the wall broke at any point, his life and his legions were over.

At the height of the crisis, Caesar sent his German cavalry on a flanking maneuver. The Gallic relief army, seeing the dust cloud of the approaching horsemen and fearing they were being surrounded, panicked and broke. The massacre that followed was absolute. The next day, Vercingetorix, dressed in his finest armor, rode out of the gates of Alesia. He circled Caesar's tribunal, dismounted, threw his weapons at Caesar's feet, and surrendered in silence. The Gallic rebellion was over. Alesia was the end of Celtic independence and the beginning of Roman Gaul. As Caesar looked at the defeated king, he felt no triumph, only the cold recognition of a job finally finished. The campaign for Gaul was over, but the campaign for Rome was about to begin.

Chapter 3: The Global War (50 BC – 46 BC)

By the winter of 50 BC, the silence in the Roman Senate was not one of peace, but of a held breath. The decade of blood in Gaul had ended, but in its wake, it had left a political landscape that was fundamentally broken. The city of Rome remained a sprawling labyrinth of marble and misery, but the men who walked its streets knew that the center could no longer hold. The triumvirate was gone. Crassus, the man of gold, lay in a nameless grave in the Parthian sands, his mouth allegedly stuffed with molten metal by his executioners—a symbolic execution that mocked his legendary greed. Julia, the daughter of Caesar and the wife of Pompey, had died in childbirth, taking with her the last biological tether between the two most powerful men in the world. Without her, the rivalry that had been managed through familial ties now stood naked and raw.

The political stalemate had reached a point of absolute stasis. In the Senate house, the *Optimates*, led by the unyielding Cato the Younger, had finally backed Caesar into a corner. They issued a *senatus consultum ultimum*—an emergency decree that effectively declared Caesar an enemy of the state if he did not lay down his command. For Caesar, this was not merely a legal dispute; it was a death warrant. He understood the machinery of Roman law perfectly; without the protection of his office (*imperium*), he would be prosecuted for his actions in Gaul, stripped of his wealth, and likely exiled or executed. To the man who had conquered the north and expanded the borders of the world, the choice was between personal annihilation and the destruction of the Republic.

The Threshold of the Rubicon

In January of 49 BC, Caesar stood on the banks of the Rubicon, a small, unremarkable stream that marked the boundary between his province of Cisalpine Gaul and the sacred soil of Italy. In the Roman mind, this stream was a metaphysical barrier. To cross it with an army was the ultimate act of treason—a declaration of war against the gods and the state. The water was shallow, likely choked with winter silt, yet it carried the weight of five hundred years of tradition.

It is easy to imagine Caesar as a figure of cold, robotic certainty, but the accounts of that night suggest a man gripped by the magnitude of what he was about to do. He reportedly stopped his carriage, pacing in the darkness as his small vanguard of the Thirteenth Legion waited nearby. These were his "Larks," men who had followed him through the forests of Germany and the mists of Britain. He knew that the moment his horse's hooves hit the water on the southern bank, the world he had grown up in would cease to exist. He turned to his officers and remarked, *"If I refrain from this crossing, I am undone; if I make it, I bring calamity upon the whole world."* The psychological weight was not just on his own soul, but on the very definition of what it meant to be Roman.

Then, with a characteristic burst of *celeritas*, he made his decision. He didn't offer a prayer for peace or a sacrifice to the old gods of the Senate. He famously uttered the words, *"Alea iacta est"*—the die is cast. It was the language of the gaming tables in the Subura, the talk of a gambler who had spent his life betting on his own survival. By the time the sun rose, the Rubicon had been crossed. He was no longer a governor; he was a rebel. The news rippled through Italy with the speed of a shockwave, traveling faster than the official couriers could manage. In Rome, the terror was absolute. The Senate had expected Caesar to pause, to negotiate, to wait for his other legions to arrive from the north. Instead, he was descending upon the city with a single legion, moving with a velocity that defied all military logic.

Pompey, the "Great" general who had once boasted that he need only stamp his foot to raise an army in Italy, found himself caught in a logistical nightmare. He realized that the city of Rome, with its porous walls and panicked population, was indefensible against a man like Caesar. In a move that stunned the populace and shattered the confidence of his supporters, Pompey ordered the evacuation of the city. He abandoned the treasury, the Senate, and the sacred hearths of Rome, fleeing south toward the port of Brundisium. He was not retreating; he was conceding the heart of the Republic to save its body. Caesar entered Rome not as a conqueror, but as a man walking into a ghost town. The silence of the Forum, usually a cacophony of commerce and law, was his first victory, but he knew the war had only just begun.

The Calculated Audacity

The opening months of the Civil War were a masterclass in what historians call Caesar's "calculated audacity." He lacked a navy, and his enemies controlled the grain supplies of the Mediterranean, holding the keys to the city's stomach. To most commanders, this would have dictated a cautious, defensive strategy, a consolidation of power within the Italian peninsula. Caesar did the opposite. He understood that the Roman people, and more importantly his own soldiers, were mesmerized by the "Luck of Caesar"—the idea that the universe itself was aligned with his success.

This belief was pushed to its limit during his attempt to cross the Adriatic to face Pompey in Greece. The sea was blockaded by Pompey's superior fleet, and the winter storms were at their peak, turning the water into a churning gray abyss. Caesar, growing impatient with the slow arrival of his reinforcements under Mark Antony, reportedly attempted to cross the sea in a small, twelve-oared skiff disguised as a slave. The desperation of the act spoke to his internal clock; he felt every minute of delay as a personal failure. When the pilot, terrified by the mountainous waves and the howling wind, tried to turn back, Caesar grabbed him by the arm and shouted into the gale: *"Fear not! You carry Caesar and his luck!"*

The skiff was forced back by the storm, but the story spread like wildfire through the ranks. It was a brilliant piece of psychological warfare, even if it had been born of genuine frustration. He was framing himself as a man of destiny, a commander who could command the elements themselves. This propaganda was essential because, on the ground, his situation was increasingly desperate. He had pursued Pompey to Dyrrachium, where he attempted a feat of engineering that bordered on the impossible: blockading a much larger army with a much smaller one. He built a massive line of fortifications, a double ring of wood and earth similar to those at Alesia, but Pompey was not a Gaul. He was a Roman general who understood Roman engineering. Pompey broke through the lines at their weakest point, handing Caesar a rare and stinging defeat. For the first time, the "Luck of Caesar" seemed to have run out. Caesar was forced to retreat into the interior of Greece, his men starving and exhausted, eating bread made from crushed roots to survive. Pompey followed, pressured by the aristocrats in his camp who were already arguing over who would get Caesar's gardens, his villas, and his priesthoods once he was dead.

Pharsalus and the Strategy of Mercy

In August of 48 BC, on the sun-baked plains of Pharsalus in central Greece, the two worlds of Rome finally collided. The air was thick with the smell of dry grass and the metallic tang of polished iron. This was not just a battle between two men; it was a battle between two different philosophies of war. Pompey's army was the traditional Roman machine—heavy, numerous, and backed by the prestige of the Senate. He had 45,000 infantry and 7,000 cavalry, nearly double what Caesar could bring to the field. Pompey's plan was simple and structurally sound: he would use his massive cavalry to sweep around Caesar's right flank, crush his outnumbered horsemen, and then roll up the infantry from the side.

Caesar, standing on the opposite ridge in his signature red cloak, saw the trap as it formed. He knew his cavalry, though battle-hardened, could not hold against Pompey's overwhelming numbers. He needed an evolution, a tactical shift that Pompey's more rigid mind would not anticipate. He took six cohorts from his rear—roughly 2,000 men—and formed them into a "hidden fourth line," positioned behind his right flank and concealed by the dust and the terrain. He gave these men a specific, brutal order that subverted the traditional training of a legionary. He told them not to throw their javelins as they usually did. Instead, they were to use them as pikes, aiming directly at the faces of Pompey's young, aristocratic cavalrymen. *"Aim for their eyes,"* he reportedly said, a psychological strike as much as a physical one. He knew that the pampered sons of the Roman elite would fear a facial scar more than a wound to the chest; to them, beauty and status were intertwined.

The battle began with a roar that could be heard for miles across the plain. As expected, Pompey's cavalry charged with the confidence of their numbers. Caesar's own horsemen gave ground, drawing the enemy into the killing zone. Then, the hidden fourth line stepped out from the dust. They didn't retreat; they lunged forward, stabbing upward at the eyes and throats of the horsemen. The shock was total. The cavalry, blinded and panicked by the unconventional tactic, turned and fled, trampling their own infantry in their haste to escape the pikes.

With the flank exposed, Caesar's veterans—men who had spent eight years in the mud of Gaul and had become a singular, lethal organism—slashed into the side of Pompey's legions. This was the moment where the professionalization of the army, begun by Marius and perfected by Caesar, showed its true lethality. These were not men fighting for a constitution or an abstract Republic; they were men fighting for the man in the red cloak who had shared their bread and their hardships. The Pompeian line didn't just break; it evaporated. Pompey, seeing his cavalry flee and his line collapse, reportedly went into his tent in a state of catatonic shock, took off his general's insignia, and fled the field on a fast horse. He left behind his army, his reputation, and the Republic he had sworn to protect, leaving his camp to be looted by the very man he had intended to destroy.

The aftermath of Pharsalus was a scene of industrial-scale slaughter, a grim reminder of the cost of civil ambition. Caesar's men moved through the enemy camp, finding tables set with silver, garlands of flowers, and wine chilled in snow—the trappings of a victory the aristocrats thought was already their birthright. But Caesar's reaction was one of grim reflection rather than jubilation. As he walked among the thousands of dead Roman citizens, his fellow countrymen, he was heard to mutter, *"They would have it so."* It was a masterful internal pivot; he was shifting the blame from his own ambition to the stubbornness of his rivals.

It was here that Caesar implemented his most effective political tool: *Clementia*, or Mercy. In the previous generation, Sulla had won his civil war and then methodically murdered every one of his opponents in the proscriptions, creating a legacy of fear. Caesar understood that this cycle of violence was a dead end. If he wanted to rule a city, he couldn't rule a graveyard. He began to pardon his enemies, including Marcus Brutus and Cicero. This was a tactical decision of the highest order, designed to neutralize the opposition. By pardoning his enemies, he was placing them under a *beneficium*—a debt of honor. In the Roman code, a man who owed his life to another was socially and morally subservient to him. *Clementia* was a way of conquering the

Senate without firing a shot, but it carried a hidden poison. The common people loved him for his restraint, but the aristocrats he pardoned felt a simmering, humiliated rage. They felt the weight of his "mercy" like a yoke around their necks, a constant reminder that their lives were a gift from a man they considered an equal, not a master.

The Egyptian Entanglement

Pompey the Great fled across the Mediterranean, his influence crumbling with every mile. He eventually sought refuge in Egypt, the last great independent kingdom of the East. The kingdom of the Ptolemies was currently gripped by a dynastic civil war between the young King Ptolemy XIII and his sister-wife, Cleopatra VII. When Pompey's boat reached the shore at Pelusium, he was met by Egyptian officials. As he stepped onto the sand, in front of his horrified wife and son who watched from the ship, he was stabbed in the back and decapitated. The Egyptians believed that by killing Caesar's enemy, they would win Caesar's favor and avoid a Roman intervention in their own affairs.

When Caesar arrived in Alexandria three days later, the Egyptians presented him with their prize: the severed head of Pompey the Great, preserved in salt to maintain its features. Caesar's reaction was not one of triumph. He reportedly turned his head away in disgust and wept. This was the man who had been his son-in-law, his partner in the Triumvirate, and the greatest rival of his life. To see him reduced to a salted trophy in the hands of a "barbarian" king was a violation of Roman dignity that Caesar could not tolerate. It was an insult to the Roman name itself.

Caesar entered Alexandria not as a guest, but as a master. He brought only two legions—roughly 4,000 men—and took up residence in the royal palace, assuming the role of arbiter in the Egyptian civil war. It was here that he met Cleopatra. Beyond the romantic legends of carpets and laundry bags, the meeting was a collision of two world-class intellects. Caesar found in Cleopatra a mind that matched his own—ambitious, culturally sophisticated, and utterly ruthless. She was a political ally who could provide the grain and wealth of Egypt to a man who was still deeply in debt from his years of bribing the Roman mob.

The Alexandrian War that followed was a claustrophobic, urban nightmare. Caesar found himself besieged in the palace district by the much larger Egyptian army. The fighting was street-to-street, house-to-house, a far cry from the open plains of Pharsalus. At one point, to prevent the Egyptian fleet from capturing the harbor and cutting off his escape, Caesar ordered his men to set fire to the docks. The fire spread uncontrollably, consuming the Egyptian fleet and, according to ancient sources, a significant portion of the Great Library of Alexandria. To the world, this was a cultural catastrophe; to Caesar, it was a tactical necessity. In his subsequent reports, he positioned himself as the beleaguered hero defending Roman interests, minimizing the cultural loss in favor of military survival.

During the height of the siege, Caesar was forced to jump into the harbor and swim for his life when his boat was swamped by retreating soldiers. Even in this moment of near-death, he maintained his sense of theater. He reportedly swam with one hand, holding his precious war commentaries above the water with the other to keep them dry, his purple general's cloak clutched in his teeth. It was a scene designed for the history books—the indomitable commander who could not be drowned by the tides of fate or the weight of his own ambition. He eventually broke the siege with the arrival of reinforcements, defeating Ptolemy XIII in a final battle on the Nile, leaving the young king to drown in the river under the weight of his golden armor.

The Cultural Clash of the East

The time Caesar spent in Egypt was a profound cultural shock that altered his vision for Rome. In Alexandria, he saw a different kind of power than the messy, litigious world of the Forum. He saw the Ptolemies living as living gods, their authority absolute and their wealth beyond the dreams of any Roman senator. He saw the Great Lighthouse, the tomb of Alexander the Great, and the sprawling complexity of a bureaucracy that had managed the Nile for three thousand years. This Egyptian influence began to seep into his own thinking, providing a template for a more centralized, autocratic rule.

He spent months on a royal barge, traveling up the Nile with Cleopatra. As they sailed past the monuments of the Pharaohs, he observed the architecture of permanence—temples and statues built to last millennia. He saw that a single man could be the state, not through debate or consensus, but through divine right. This was a seductive vision for a man who had spent his life fighting the obstructionism of the Senate. When he finally left Egypt in 47 BC, having secured Cleopatra's throne and left her pregnant with his son, Caesarion, he was a changed man. He had seen a vision of a world where power was not debated, but worshipped.

His return to the West was a whirlwind of activity, a demonstration of his trademark speed. On his way back to Italy, he detoured into Asia Minor to deal with Pharnaces II, who had seized the opportunity of the Roman civil war to reclaim his father's empire. Caesar met him at Zela. The battle was not a struggle; it was an execution. It lasted only four hours. It was so swift and so decisive that Caesar sent a three-word dispatch to the Senate that has become the ultimate summary of his career: *"Veni, Vidi, Vici"*—I came, I saw, I conquered. It was a masterpiece of PR, a reminder to the men in Rome that while they had been talking and plotting, he had been winning. He was no longer just a general; he was the master of the world's clock, a man who could settle a kingdom's fate in an afternoon.

The Weight of the Crown and the Calendar

By 46 BC, the Civil War was nearly over, but the final embers were the most difficult to extinguish. The remnants of the Pompeian faction had fled to North Africa, where they had allied themselves with King Juba of Numidia. Caesar followed them into the desert, facing a grueling campaign against an enemy that used hit-and-run tactics and scorched-earth policies. At the Battle of Thapsus, his legions, frustrated by years of war and the perceived softness of their commander's *Clementia*, ignored his orders to spare the enemy. They slaughtered 50,000 Pompeians in a frenzy of pent-up rage. It was a sign that even Caesar could not always control the monster he had created; the legions had become his instrument, but they had also become a law unto themselves.

When news of the victory reached Rome, the Senate, now purged of its most vocal critics and terrified of the survivors, voted him honors that bordered on the divine. They made him Dictator for ten years, an unprecedented term that effectively ended the Republic's tradition of short-term magistracies. They renamed the month of Quintilis to "Julius," placing his name among the seasons. They allowed him to wear the triumphal dress—the purple robe and the laurel wreath—on all public occasions, a constant visual reminder of his supremacy.

One of Caesar's most enduring acts during this period was a reform that was not military, but intellectual: the reform of time itself. For centuries, the Roman calendar had been a mess of political manipulation. The priests would add "intercalary" months at their whim, often to extend the terms of their friends or cut short the terms of their enemies. By 46 BC, the calendar was so out of sync with the seasons that the harvest festivals were being celebrated in the spring. Drawing on the astronomical knowledge he had acquired in Alexandria, Caesar introduced the Julian Calendar. He abolished the lunar system and replaced it with a solar one of 365 days. To fix the existing discrepancy, he decreed that the year 46 BC would have 445 days—the "Year of Confusion."

This was the ultimate expression of his power. He was not just ruling the people; he was ruling the sun and the stars. He was imposing Roman order on the very fabric of existence. Cicero joked that the stars now only rose by Caesar's decree, but for the average citizen, it was a practical miracle. It was a sign that the chaos of the old Republic was being replaced by the predictable, rational authority of a single mind. Caesar was no longer just a man of history; he was the man who had defined how history would be measured. His fingerprints were now on the very days and months of every citizen's life.

Caesar returned to Rome in 46 BC to celebrate four consecutive Triumphs: for Gaul, Egypt, Pontus, and Africa. It was a spectacle of wealth and power that the city had never seen. Thousands of captives were paraded through the streets, followed by wagons loaded with gold, silver, and the exotic animals of the south—elephants, giraffes, and leopards. But as the silver eagles of the legions passed the Rostra, many Romans noticed a subtle shift in the atmosphere. The soldiers weren't singing songs about the Republic or the glory of Rome; they were singing ribald, mocking verses about their general's sex life and his "luck." They were his men, not the state's. Caesar sat in his chariot, the slave standing behind him whispering the traditional warning, *"Remember you are mortal,"* but the words seemed increasingly hollow in the face of such absolute adulation.

The Architect in his House

As he sat in the newly built Forum Iulium—a massive project funded by the spoils of Gaul and designed to dwarf the old Forum Romanum—Caesar looked at the temple he had dedicated to Venus Genetrix, his divine ancestor. The forum was a statement of intent, a new center of gravity for the city. He was sixty years old. He was at the height of his powers, but he was increasingly isolated by his own success. His health was failing, his fits were becoming more frequent and public, and he found himself surrounded by men who either worshipped him with a sycophancy that disgusted him or wanted him dead with a fervor that he couldn't ignore.

He had won the world, but he had lost the city he loved. The old camaraderie of the Subura was gone, replaced by the stiff protocols of a court. He had become the center of a new universe, a man around whom everything revolved, yet he was a man who had no peers. He had pardoned his enemies, but in doing so, he had ensured they would never forget their humiliation. He had enriched his friends, but in doing so, he had made them targets for those who felt overlooked. The die had been cast, the river had been crossed, and now, the architect of chaos had to live in the house he had built—a house that felt more like a tomb with every passing day.

He had saved the city from the immediate chaos of civil war, but he had done so by becoming the very thing the Romans had spent five hundred years trying to prevent: a king. He had replaced the fragile, beautiful, and often corrupt consensus of the Republic with the cold efficiency of a single will. As he looked out over the city from his gardens across the Tiber, he knew that his work was unfinished. He was already planning a massive campaign against the Parthians in the East, a new war to provide a new distraction. But the global war had been won, and the war for the soul of Caesar—and the future of Rome—was now entering its final, tragic act. The shadows in the Senate were growing longer, and the knives, once used to carve up the world, were now being sharpened for the man who had claimed it all.

Chapter 4: The Perpetual Dictator (45 BC – 44 BC)

By the spring of 45 BC, the Roman world had reached a state of exhaustion. The fires that had been lit on the banks of the Rubicon four years earlier had scorched the earth from the forests of Gaul to the deserts of Numidia. The oceans were littered with the wreckage of Roman ships, and the soil of three continents was enriched by the blood of Roman citizens. When Caesar returned to the city after his final, brutal victory over the sons of Pompey at Munda in Spain, he did not return to the Rome of his youth. He returned to a city that was hollowed out, its institutions shattered, and its people waiting with a mixture of adoration and profound, silent dread.

Caesar was now the sole master of the Mediterranean. He was the *Dictator Perpetuo*—the Dictator in Perpetuity. This was a title that struck at the very heart of the Roman identity. In the old world, the dictatorship was a temporary emergency measure, a brief suspension of liberty to save the state. By making it perpetual, Caesar had effectively declared that the emergency would never end, or rather, that he was the only one capable of managing the permanent crisis of the Roman soul. He moved through the city not as a magistrate, but as a force of nature. He was fifty-five years old, his hair thinning, his face lined with the stresses of a decade of constant warfare, yet he was possessed by a manic, restless energy. He was a man in a hurry, acting as if he could feel the shadow of the Ides lengthening behind him.

The Administrative Sprint

In these final months, Caesar engaged in what historians call an "administrative sprint." He was attempting to rebuild a centuries-old civilization in the span of a few months. He was everywhere at once—drafting laws to settle his veterans, planning the drainage of the Pontine Marshes, proposing a canal through the Isthmus of Corinth, and designing a massive new public library that would rival the one he had burned in Alexandria. To Caesar, the state was a tactical problem to be solved with the same cold, geometric logic he had used at Alesia. He saw the inefficiency of the old Republic—the endless debating, the bribery, the gridlock—and he sought to replace it with the clean lines of a singular will.

One of his most profound acts of "soft power" was the final implementation and refinement of the Julian Calendar. To the modern mind, a calendar is a neutral tool, but to the Romans, it was the rhythm of their lives, the schedule of their festivals, and the structure of their religion. By taking control of time, Caesar was demonstrating that his authority was not just political, but cosmic. He was the *Pontifex Maximus*, the high priest of Rome, and he was imposing order on the stars themselves. He felt a deep, intellectual satisfaction in this reform; it was a victory over chaos that required no legions. Yet, to the Senate, this was the ultimate arrogance. He was telling them that even the sun and the moon now moved by his leave.

This friction was not limited to the stars. Caesar's settling of his veterans was a masterstroke of social engineering that simultaneously solved a military problem and a poverty crisis. He didn't just give them land; he founded new Roman colonies at Carthage and Corinth—cities that Rome had destroyed a century earlier. He was rebuilding the world in his own image. But to do this, he had to bypass the Senate entirely. He made decisions in his private study, surrounded by his secretaries and his

Greek intellectuals, while the senators waited in his antechamber like common petitioners. He could feel their resentment, a thick, palpable heat in the room, but he found he no longer cared for the delicate dance of Republican etiquette. He had seen the efficiency of the Ptolemies; he had seen how a god-king could move a world. The slow, grinding gears of the Roman constitution now felt to him like an insult to his intelligence.

The Gilded Chair and the Purple Robe

As 44 BC began, Caesar's internal state began to drift further from the traditional Roman center. He was no longer the man of the people who shared the mud of Gaul with his soldiers; he was becoming a figure of remote, almost alien majesty. He began to appear in public wearing the long, all-purple robe of the ancient kings and the triumphal laurel wreath. He sat in a gilded chair in the Senate house, elevated above his peers. Most tellingly, he did not rise when the Senate approached him with a list of new honors. This was not just a lapse in manners; it was a profound failure of his once-impeccable PR touch.

The "Gilded Chair" was more than a piece of furniture; it was a throne in all but name. Caesar's internal thoughts during this period seem to have been a mix of impatience and a growing contempt for the men who surrounded him. He saw the senators as sycophants who had voted him divine honors while secretly sharpening their daggers. He knew they hated him, but he believed that their fear and their self-interest would keep them in check. He miscalculated the one thing a Roman aristocrat valued more than life: *dignitas*. By refusing to rise, by wearing the robes of a king, he was stripping them of their status, treating them as subjects rather than fellow citizens.

His propaganda machine worked overtime to manage this growing rift, but it was becoming increasingly clumsy. He placed his own image on the coinage—the first living Roman ever to do so. To the common man in the street, this was a sign of stability, a promise that the civil wars were over. But to the elite, it was the face of a tyrant. Caesar seemed to be testing the limits of what the Roman psyche could endure. He was an experimenter, a man who had always lived on the edge of the possible, and he was now applying that same experimentalism to the concept of monarchy. He wanted to know if Rome could be a kingdom in reality while remaining a Republic in name. He was looking for the breaking point, and he was about to find it.

The Lupercalia Experiment

The most famous of these experiments occurred in February of 44 BC, during the festival of the Lupercalia. It was a day of ancient, wild ritual, where young men ran through the streets of Rome clad in goatskins. Caesar sat on his gilded chair on the Rostra, watching the festivities. Mark Antony, Caesar's loyal lieutenant and a man of visceral, impulsive energy, approached the Rostra and attempted to place a diadem—the white ribbon of a Hellenistic king—on Caesar's head.

The crowd's reaction was a sudden, icy silence. In that moment, Caesar felt the limits of his power. He saw that while the people loved him as a protector, they still recoiled from the word "King." He pushed the diadem away, and the crowd erupted in cheers. Antony tried a second time, and again the silence fell. Caesar, ever the master of the public moment, finally ordered the crown to be taken to the Temple of Jupiter, declaring, *"Jupiter alone is King of the Romans."*

This was a staged event, a carefully choreographed piece of political theater designed to gauge the public's appetite for a formal monarchy. Caesar had his answer: the people weren't ready. But the damage was done. To the conspirators—men like Cassius and the high-minded Brutus—the Lupercalia was not a rejection of kingship; it was a rehearsal for it. They saw the theater for what it was. They realized that Caesar was not going to stop. He was planning a three-year campaign in the East against the Parthians, and they knew that if he returned with the spoils of the Orient, his power would be truly untouchable. They were running out of time. The experiment had backfired, and the "Luck of Caesar" was finally starting to turn into a trap of his own making.

The Calculated Audacity of Death

In the final weeks of his life, Caesar made a decision that has baffled historians for two millennia: he dismissed his Spanish bodyguard. He walked the streets of Rome with only his lictors, entirely vulnerable to any man with a hidden blade. To some, this was the ultimate arrogance—the belief that his person was sacred, that no Roman would dare to strike the man who had saved the state. But a deeper analysis, particularly that of historians like Freeman, suggests a more calculated, darker audacity.

Caesar was tired. He was suffering from increasing bouts of "the falling sickness," and his once-unbreakable constitution was fraying. He was a man who had always lived for his reputation, for his *fama*. He may have realized that a long, slow decline into senility or a paranoid, bunker-bound dictatorship would ruin the masterpiece of his life. He chose, instead, a short and glorious death over a long and miserable one. He reportedly said that he had lived long enough for both nature and for glory. By dismissing his guards, he was inviting fate to do its worst. He was placing his life back onto the gaming table, one last bet on how he would be remembered.

On the morning of the Ides of March, 44 BC, the omens were screaming. His wife, Calpurnia, had dreamed of his death; a soothsayer had warned him of the day; and even his own body seemed to rebel as he felt the onset of another fit. He almost stayed home. But Decimus Brutus, one of the conspirators he trusted most, arrived at his house and mocked his fears, urging him not to keep the Senate waiting. Caesar, ever sensitive to the charge of cowardice, dressed and headed for the Theatre of Pompey, where the Senate was meeting.

He walked into the hall, a man alone among his enemies. He sat in his gilded chair, and the conspirators crowded around him under the pretext of a petition. Tillius Cimber grabbed his purple robe, pulling it from his shoulders—the signal for the attack. The first blow, from Casca, was clumsy, catching him near the neck. Caesar turned with the speed of a soldier, stabbing Casca with his stylus, shouting, *"Scoundrel, Casca, what are you doing?"*

But then the rest of the daggers came out. He saw the faces of the men he had pardoned, the men he had enriched, and finally, he saw Marcus Brutus—the man who was rumored to be his own son. In that moment, the accounts say he stopped fighting. He didn't offer a final speech; he simply pulled his purple robe over his head, shielding his face so that his enemies would not see him die. He fell at the base of the statue of Pompey the Great, his old rival's cold stone eyes looking down at the bloody heap on the floor.

Twenty-three wounds had ended the life of the man, but they had birthed the myth. The conspirators ran into the streets shouting of "Liberty," but they found only a terrified silence. They had killed the Dictator, but they had not killed the problem he had solved. By removing the one man capable of holding the world together, they had ensured that the fires would burn for another thirteen years. Caesar had died as he lived—through a calculated act of audacity—leaving behind a house that was now truly empty, waiting for a new architect to build something even more formidable upon his ruins.

Chapter 5: The Caesarean Synthesis

To walk through the ruins of the Roman Forum today is to walk through a landscape of ghosts, but none looms larger than the man whose funeral pyre once lit up the night sky near the Regia. When we look back across the abyss of two millennia, we often see Julius Caesar as a statue—cold, marble-white, and inevitable. But the Caesar of history was not a statue; he was a master of fluidity, a man who lived in the friction between the old world of the Senate and the new world of the Empire. He was the architect of a synthesis that took the fractured pieces of the Roman Republic and fused them into a singular, lethal engine of power.

To understand how a single human being could collapse a five-hundred-year-old system and replace it with himself, we must decode the three fundamental traits that defined his life: his audacity as a strategic weapon, his mastery of the media, and his ability to integrate the battlefield with the courtroom. This was the "Caesarean Synthesis"—a blueprint for power that did not just change Rome, but created the very concept of the West.

I. Audacity as Strategy: The Psychology of the Gap

If there is one thread that connects the young man defying Sulla in the streets of Rome to the master of the world crossing the Rubicon, it is a psychological phenomenon we might call the "Psychology of the Gap." Caesar succeeded throughout his life because he operated in the space where his opponents believed action was impossible. He understood, perhaps better than any man in history, that the greatest limitation on human action is not physical, but mental. In the rigid, tradition-bound world of the Roman aristocracy, behavior was governed by a set of unwritten rules—the *mos maiorum*. Caesar's genius lay in his realization that these rules were only as strong as the collective will to enforce them. He saw that the Senate functioned on the assumption of a shared reality, a mutual agreement on what was "done" and what was "not done." Caesar, however, looked at the chessboard and realized he could simply pick up the pieces and move them in ways the rules didn't allow.

In Chapter 1, we saw this in his refusal to divorce his wife at Sulla's command. To the

Roman elite of the time, Sulla was an unstoppable force of nature, a man who had mastered the art of the proscription and turned the city into a slaughterhouse. To defy him was not just brave; it was considered a form of madness. But Caesar recognized a "gap" in Sulla's power—the gap between the Dictator's ability to kill and his ability to break a man's *dignitas*. By choosing potential death over submission, Caesar won a psychological victory that shielded him for the rest of his career. He understood that once you show a tyrant you do not fear death, you become a variable they cannot calculate. This early act of defiance wasn't just about a marriage; it was a laboratory for the rest of his life, proving that the established order was far more fragile than it appeared. It taught him that the "impossible" is often just a social construct.

This audacity reached its military zenith at Alesia, as described in Chapter 2. When Caesar built his double line of fortifications, he was operating in a space that defied every rule of ancient warfare. He was simultaneously the besieger and the besieged, a paradoxical position that should have led to his annihilation. To his Gallic enemies, the idea of a Roman army locking itself in a wooden cage between two massive forces was absurd. They waited for the Romans to panic, to break, or to retreat. But Caesar lived in that gap of uncertainty. He knew that if he could hold the center, the sheer psychological weight of his refusal to move would eventually shatter the morale of the relief army. He didn't just fight the Gauls; he fought their conception of what was possible. He leveraged the claustrophobia of the siege to create a pressure cooker where only his own discipline remained constant. This willingness to endure extreme vulnerability for the sake of a strategic trap became his signature. He thrived in the "no-man's-land" of risk where more cautious men saw only death.

This was not "recklessness," though his enemies often called it that to comfort themselves. It was a calculated understanding of human inertia. Most men, even great men like Pompey, wait for the "right" moment—the moment when the logistics are settled, the omens are good, and the law is on their side. Caesar realized that by acting *before* that moment, he could seize a momentum that no amount of preparation could overcome. When he crossed the Rubicon with a single legion, as we explored in Chapter 3, he wasn't just gambling; he was exploiting the gap between the Senate's decree and their ability to enforce it. While they were still debating the legalities of his command in the comfort of their villas, he was already at their gates. He understood that in the theater of power, speed is the ultimate form of legitimacy. This "speed" was as much cognitive as it was physical; he out-thought his rivals by refusing to acknowledge the barriers they took for granted. He created "facts on the ground" that made their debates irrelevant. By the time the Senate had decided on a course of action, Caesar had already changed the environment in which that action would take place.

The implications of this "Psychology of the Gap" were profound for the future of Rome. It demonstrated that a singular, decisive will could overrule a thousand years of consensus if it moved faster than the consensus could react. This realization created a permanent fracture in the Roman psyche. It meant that henceforth, safety lay only in being the first to strike, a lesson that would fuel centuries of subsequent civil wars. Caesar had exposed the central weakness of the Republic: that it was a system built on trust and delay, two things he had no intention of respecting. He showed that the law is only a barrier if you allow it to be, and in doing so, he taught every ambitious man who followed him that the only real rule is power.

II. The Media Strategist: Latin as a Siege Engine

While Caesar's swords won him provinces, it was his pen that won him immortality. He was perhaps the first truly modern media strategist, a man who understood that in a sprawling empire, the narrative of the war is as important as the war itself. He used the Latin language not as a medium of expression, but as a siege engine designed to batter down the skepticism of the Roman public. He understood that for a general in the field, the most dangerous enemy is not the one in front of him, but the one behind him in the Senate house, whispering in the ears of the voters. To combat this, he created a literary style that was as disciplined and lethal as his legions.

His *Commentarii de Bello Gallico* (Commentaries on the Gallic War) are a masterclass in psychological manipulation disguised as plain reporting. By writing in the third person—referring to himself always as "Caesar"—he achieved a tone of detached, objective authority. He wasn't telling you his opinion; he was telling you what "Caesar" had done, as if he were an impartial observer recording the movements of a force of nature. This stripped away the appearance of ego, making his most self-serving actions seem like historical necessity. When he describes the slaughter of the Helvetii or the bridge across the Rhine, he does so with the cold clarity of an engineer. This was designed to neutralize the moral objections of his critics in Rome. How could one argue against a man who presented his massacres as mere logistical updates? He was reframing his own ambition as a series of inevitable, logical responses to external threats.

Think back to the description of his crossing to Britain in Chapter 2. He doesn't describe the terror of the storm or the uncertainty of the landing in the flowery, adjective-heavy prose typical of the period. Instead, he uses a style that is direct, sparse, and muscular— a style known as *Atticism*. He describes the tides, the placement of the ships, and the engineering of the bridges with a geometric precision. This was a deliberate PR weapon. By presenting himself as a rational, clear-headed administrator of violence, he was reassuring the Roman middle class—the equestrians and the merchants—that their interests were in safe hands. He was the "fixer," the man who brought order to the chaos of the "barbarian" north. He transformed himself from a politician into a personification of Roman efficiency, a man who did not seek power but was simply the most qualified to hold it. He understood that the Roman people were weary of the chaotic, emotive politics of the Forum; they wanted a man who could speak the language of results.

Furthermore, Caesar understood the power of the "Soundbite" long before the term existed. His most famous phrases—*Alea iacta est* (The die is cast) and *Veni, Vidi, Vici* (I came, I saw, I conquered)—were not just spontaneous outbursts. They were carefully crafted branding. They were short, rhythmic, and impossible to forget. They traveled through the streets of Rome like a virus, simplifying complex geopolitical realities into a singular narrative of his own inevitability. He was weaponizing the language of the Republic to build the foundations of a monarchy. Every dispatch he sent from Gaul was a brick in the monument he was building to himself, ensuring that by the time he returned to Rome, the public had already lived through his victories in their imagination. He had conquered the Roman mind long before he re-entered the city's gates, turning his readers into his involuntary accomplices. He understood that whoever controls the vocabulary of a conflict ultimately controls its outcome.

The consequence of this media mastery was the birth of "Caesarism"—a political reality where the leader's public image is as vital to his power as his actual commands. He set the standard for the *Princeps*, the "first citizen" who rules through a carefully managed facade of Republican modesty. He taught his successors that the secret to absolute power is to never call it by its name. By using the plain language of the camp and the ledger, he made the unthinkable seem mundane. He stripped the "monarchy" of its crowns and scepters and replaced them with the bureaucratic language of "reports" and "necessity." In doing so, he created a template for modern authoritarianism: the leader who rules not as a king, but as the ultimate public servant, a man whose power is supposedly derived from his unique ability to "get things done."

III. The Integrated Tactician: The Unified Field of Power

The third pillar of the Caesarean Synthesis was his ability to integrate disparate fields of human activity into a single, unified strategy. Most Romans of his era were specialists: they were either great lawyers like Cicero, or great generals like Pompey. Caesar refused to accept this division. He realized that the battlefield, the courtroom, the grain market, and the bedroom were all part of the same theater of operations. He viewed the world as a unified field of power where a victory in one sector could be leveraged for a breakthrough in another. This was the "total war" of the Roman mind, where politics was simply warfare by other means, and vice versa.

In Chapter 3, we examined his campaign in Egypt. A traditional general would have focused solely on the military relief of Alexandria. But Caesar understood that the political survival of Cleopatra and the grain supply of the Roman mob were inextricably linked to his military position. He managed the logistics of a siege while simultaneously managing a romantic and political alliance that would fund his future wars. He was, as historians like Adrian Goldsworthy have noted, a master of logistics—but as Freeman points out, he was equally a master of human emotion. He could calculate the weight of a grain shipment and the weight of a queen's ambition with the same terrifying accuracy. This multifaceted approach made him impossible to predict, as he was never playing just one game. He was playing the long game of dynastic security while fighting for his life in the short game of urban combat.

This integration allowed him to perform what we called the "Administrative Sprint" in Chapter 4. When he reformed the calendar, he wasn't just being a nerd for astronomy; he was performing a military operation on the concept of time. He saw that the chaos of the Roman calendar was a tactical weakness that his enemies used to manipulate elections and legal terms. By fixing the year to 365 days, he was performing a "soft power" sweep of the entire Roman world, imposing his own sense of order on every farm, every market, and every temple in the Empire. He unified the measurement of time just as he had unified the command of the legions. He realized that to control a people, you must control the rhythm of their lives, making himself the silent conductor of the Roman heartbeat. This was the ultimate expression of the "Integrated Tactician"—the man who could command the seasons themselves to march in step with his political goals.

This ability to manage logistics and emotion simultaneously is perhaps most evident in his policy of *Clementia*. As we explored in the context of Pharsalus, Caesar's mercy was not an emotional outburst; it was a cold, tactical integration of ethics into his broader strategy. He realized that a dead enemy is a martyr, but a pardoned enemy is a client. He was using the courtroom tactic of "the debt of honor" and applying it to the battlefield. He was "buying" the future loyalty of the state with the lives of the men he had just defeated. This unified approach meant that Caesar was never "off duty." Whether he was presiding over a trial or crossing a river in a storm, he was always calculating how each action fed into the grand synthesis of his authority. He had moved beyond the petty distinctions of civilian and military life, becoming a singular, total political entity. He understood that the Republic failed because its parts were at war with each other—the Senate vs. the People, the City vs. the Provinces. Caesar sought to end this friction by becoming the single point of convergence for all of them.

The ultimate consequence of this integrated tactics was the creation of a new kind of state—the Roman Empire. It was a system designed to be governed by a single man who could oversee everything from the price of wheat in North Africa to the movements of legions on the Rhine. Caesar had proven that such a thing was possible, but he had also proven that it was incredibly fragile, for it required a man of his specific, terrifying genius to hold it together. He had created a vacuum that only another "Caesar" could fill. By integrating every aspect of Roman life under his own person, he made the survival of the state dependent on his own survival. This was his final, most profound synthesis: he had merged his own biography with the history of the world.

In those final months before the Ides, this synthesis had reached its absolute form. He had become the center of a new universe, a man who had collapsed the old distinctions between the god and the man, the law and the will, the word and the deed. He walked the streets without guards because he believed the synthesis was so complete that no one would dare to touch its central node. He was wrong, of course. The tragedy of the Caesarean Synthesis was that it was too complete; it left no room for the very people it was built to govern. It offered efficiency at the price of dignity, and order at the price of liberty. By solving the problem of the Republic's chaos, he had created the problem of his own absolute presence. The man had become the state, and in doing so, he had ensured that his own death would be the only way for the state to breathe again.

Yet, even in death, his traits—his audacity, his media mastery, and his integrated tactics—became the DNA of every ruler who followed. The conspirators killed the man, but they could not kill the synthesis. Within a generation, the world he had envisioned would become a permanent reality. He had set the world on a new path, crossing a final Rubicon of history from which there was no returning. He had built a legacy that would haunt the Western imagination for two thousand years—from the halls of the

Vatican to the offices of modern dictators. He remains the ghost in the machine of every empire to come, a reminder of what happens when a single human will decides that the rules of the past are merely a suggestion, and the future is a blank page waiting for a single name. He was the architect of our modernity, a man who looked into the abyss of the Republic's collapse and chose to build a bridge across it using nothing but the sheer, unadulterated strength of his own character.

In the end, Caesar's life serves as a profound meditation on the nature of power. He demonstrated that true authority is not granted, but synthesised from a thousand disparate acts of will. He showed that the world belongs not to those who follow the rules, but to those who have the audacity to rewrite them in their own image. As we stand today among the broken stones of his Forum, we are not just looking at the ruins of an empire; we are looking at the footprint of a man who believed he could be everything at once. He was the conqueror and the clerk, the lover and the killer, the priest and the rebel. He was the first truly global man, a figure who understood that in a world of chaos, the only thing that endures is the synthesis of a singular mind. His funeral pyre may have gone out two millennia ago, but the heat of his ambition still warms the structures of the world we live in today. He is the eternal Dictator, the perpetual architect, and the ghost that still whispers to every man who looks at a throne and sees only an empty chair.

Conclusion: The Echo in the Stone

If we return to the Forum one final time, as the last of the tourists depart and the cicadas begin their rhythmic thrum in the dry grass, we are left with a question that history rarely answers. Was the fall of the Republic a tragedy of a few men's ambition, or was it the inevitable destiny of a system that had simply exhausted its capacity for hope? We have followed the path of Gaius Julius Caesar from the mud of the Subura to the pinnacle of a world that he broke and rebuilt in his own image. We have seen how his audacity, his mastery of the word, and his terrifyingly integrated mind became the scaffolding for a new kind of human existence. But as we stand among the shadows of the statues, the air feels thinner, more fragile.

There is a wistfulness that clings to these stones, a sense of something lost that can never be recovered. The Republic, for all its flaws—its corruption, its violence, its staggering inequality—represented a dream of collective responsibility. It was a messy, loud, and often hypocritical argument between equals. When Caesar crossed the Rubicon, he didn't just end a war; he ended that argument. He replaced the friction of the Forum with the silence of the palace. He offered the Roman people security, efficiency, and bread, and in exchange, he asked only for their agency. It is a bargain that civilizations have been making ever since, a recurring rhythm in the story of our species.

We look back at the "Caesarean Synthesis" and see the birth of the West, but we also see the closing of a door. The tragedy of Caesar is not that he was a villain, but that he was so successful. He fixed a world that was broken, but he did so by making himself indispensable, creating a void that could only be filled by other giants, other masters, other Caesars. The ruins around us are not just the remains of buildings; they are the remains of a transition. The amber light hitting the Curia today is the same light that hit it two thousand years ago, but the world it illuminates is one that Caesar built. We live in his calendar, we speak through the echoes of his language, and we still grapple with the "Psychology of the Gap" that he pioneered.

As the sun dips below the horizon and the violet shadows finally consume the Via Sacra, we are reminded that every civilization is a fragile consensus. It lives and dies by the stories it tells itself. Caesar told a story of inevitability, of order over chaos, and of the Great Man as the ultimate servant of necessity. It is a story so powerful that we are still telling it today. But as the darkness settles over the Forum, we might wonder about the voices that were silenced to make room for that narrative—the whispers of a Republic that, despite its rot, believed that no one man should ever be the sun around which the world revolves.

The boots have stopped marching. The dust has settled. The man is a ghost, and the empire he birthed is a collection of pleasing geometries for the modern eye. Yet, if you listen closely to the wind whistling through the jagged marble, you can still hear the echo of that measured, rhythmic tread. It is a reminder that history is never truly over; it is merely waiting for the next person to look at the ruins of a system and decide that they, and they alone, have the audacity to begin again. The shadows of the statues remain, watching and waiting, as the cycle of the rise and the fall prepares to turn once more.